31

Gender Identity

Other titles in the *LGBTQ Issues* series include:

Gender Identity

Olivia Ghafoerkhan

ReferencePoint
Press®

San Diego, CA

© 2021 ReferencePoint Press, Inc.
Printed in the United States

For more information, contact:
ReferencePoint Press, Inc.
PO Box 27779
San Diego, CA 92198
www.ReferencePointPress.com

OCT 2 3 2020

LIBRARY OF CONGRESS CATALOGING-IN-PUBLICATION DATA

Names: Ghafoerkhan, Olivia, 1982- author.
Title: Gender identity / by Olivia Ghafoerkhan.
Description: San Diego, CA : ReferencePoint Press, Inc., 2020. | Series:
  LGBTQ issues | Includes bibliographical references and index.
Identifiers: LCCN 2020011953 (print) | LCCN 2020011954 (ebook) | ISBN
  9781682829158 (library binding) | ISBN 9781682829165 (ebook)
Subjects: LCSH: Gender identity--Juvenile literature.
Classification: LCC HQ18.552 .G43 2020 (print) | LCC HQ18.552 (ebook) |
  DDC 305.3--dc23
LC record available at https://lccn.loc.gov/2020011953
LC ebook record available at https://lccn.loc.gov/2020011954

Contents

What Is Gender?

Gender identity and expression make up a diverse range of experiences. In previous decades those who did not identify with the gender they were assigned at birth, usually based on the appearance of external genitalia, often had to live as that gender anyway or face societal isolation. Even in situations in which transitioning, or moving toward living as one's true gender, was possible, it often came with the cost of losing one's family and friends.

Gender Variations

The world is slowly moving toward a less rigid understanding of gender. Acceptance of those who live outside the male-female gender lines is growing, but it is by no means universal. Gender in some circles is still considered binary. In this view, a person who has a male anatomy at birth is male; a person who has a female anatomy at birth is female. And for most of the world's people, this connection between anatomy and gender still holds true. But this traditional relationship does not allow for variation. What is becoming increasingly clear is that there are in fact variations in human gender. Experts are finding that gender is a complex mixture of biology, neurology, self-perception, and self-understanding. One's biological sex may or may not be the same as one's gender.

Gender identity is the term used most often to explain one's understanding of one's own gender. A person whose biological sex and gender identity align is referred to as cisgender. When this alignment between biological sex and gender identity does not exist, the person is often referred to as transgender. Some people take issue with the term *gender identity* because they feel it implies that the gender they identify as is not their "true" gender. And that does make a valid point. People do not normally say "I identify as a woman"—rather, they say, "I am a woman." But the term *gender identity* is a shorthand way to reference a person's internal sense of gender versus biological gender (meaning the gender assigned at birth).

Gender identity can be thought of as a spectrum of identities. Some people identify as male or female but others fall in different places within—or even outside—the spectrum.

A Spectrum of Identities

It helps to think of gender as a spectrum of identities rather than a binary system of only male and female. There are people who identify in all the different places within the spectrum and some who feel their identity falls outside of the spectrum altogether. Often those who do not identify as male or female will use gender-neutral pronouns like *they*, *them*, and *their* (as opposed to *his* or *her*). Mason Martinez, a college student from Long Island, struggled all through high school to figure out their identity. Mason shares:

I was unsure of many things in my life. But I was slowly realizing that I didn't identify as male or female; it's more like I've always danced between the two. . . . Unintentionally and unknowingly, I'd lived my life gender neutral. . . . I realized that I am non-binary during a conversation with my friend Finley. . . . I fall directly in the middle. Whenever people used gender-specific pronouns for me, it didn't feel either wrong or right; it felt misplaced. It left this feeling in my stomach that I never knew how to describe. . . . I never felt 100% male, or female. Talking to Fin helped me determine that being non-binary and using they/them pronouns best suited me. When I came out as Mason it was like a heavy weight was lifted off me. When I legally changed my name it felt like I was reborn. For the first time in my life I felt like I was free without being judged by anyone. . . . Now that I feel more certain about my identity, I am more comfortable speaking up about my preferred pronouns. Now that I'm in college, I have given speeches and written research papers on educating people about the difference between gender and sexuality, as well as the different genders and pronouns. I also help others through the complicated legal processes of changing your name and gender markings on official documents. Still, there are days when I wish I had my binders to help me feel more masculine. But I feel that less and less. My name is Mason Martinez and I am a proud non-binary, pansexual individual. My pronouns are they/them. When people ask me where I got my name, I stand tall and proud and say, "I picked it myself."[1]

Mason's story reveals the struggle some people have in figuring out their gender identity. It also illustrates the rich and diverse variety of gender identities and expression.

Chapter One

Finding Oneself

Parents do not often talk about gender identity with their kids, and it is not a concept that is often introduced in school. Gender-diverse people become aware—often slowly—of feeling like a gender other than the gender assigned to them at birth. This awareness comes at varying times. Often gender-diverse individuals have a feeling early in life that they are somehow different, but not everyone will recognize what this feeling means. It can take people years to "come out" or acknowledge their differences. Part of this may be that they lack the language to identify what they are experiencing. Another issue for young children is that parents may not understand what their child is experiencing. Instead of supporting a child's gender expression, parents may reinforce the gender roles and stereotypes of the child's biological sex. For example, "boys do not wear dresses, boys play with trucks" is a common enforcement of gender roles. David, age twenty-six, remembers this lack of understanding from his childhood vividly:

> I never thought of myself as a girl. I thought that one day I'd wake up and I'd be a boy and that would be the end of it. I didn't see it as a long-term thing. I remember having arguments with my mum telling me "you're not a boy and that's the end of it." And I don't remember what led up to it. And so I felt there was nothing my parents could do about it so I didn't talk to them about it. I knew who I was but no one could see that.[2]

Different Identities

For most people gender is not at all complex. A person is either male or female—a simple fact determined at birth and based on internal anatomy and external genitalia. This group, which is the largest, is known as cisgender.

For other people, however, gender is more complex than biological sex. It involves not just biology but how people understand themselves. About 3 percent of the US population does not identify with the gender they were assigned at birth. This could be a person born with female genitalia who identifies as a man. Or it could be a person born with male genitalia who identifies as a woman. These individuals are described as transgender.

For some transgender people, their gender does not fall neatly into the man or woman box. The process of classifying people as only men or women is referred to as the gender binary. While the gender binary works well for those who can easily check the

For most people gender is not at all complex. A person is either male or female—a simple fact determined at birth.

man or woman box, some people fall somewhere in between or completely outside this system. These people often identify as nonbinary. Some may identify as gender fluid, meaning their gender is not fixed at a single point. They may still refer to themselves as transgender as well. Gender expression and identity are very complex, and the language one uses to express gender identity may vary.

There are also people whose biology is neither male nor female. Intersex people are born with the sex characteristics of both genders. This could be in the form of external genitalia, internal sex organs, hormones, chromosomes, or a combination of these. It is estimated that about one in one hundred people are born with an intersex condition.

Early Experiences

Children are often unaware of gender identity and gender diversity. They do not have the words to put to their feelings. Christina, a fashion designer who shared her story in the book *Beyond Magenta: Transgender Teens Speak Out*, talked about how she experienced gender as a small child. Christina's experience shows how a lack of language at an early age can be a barrier:

"When I was born, I was named Matthew. Early on, when I was little, I felt that I wanted to be a girl, but I didn't have a full understanding about it. I knew I was a boy because my mom and dad told me I was one."[3]

Sometimes feelings of being assigned the wrong gender can be really strong. This can sometimes be diagnosed as gender dysphoria. Gender dysphoria is the name for the distress individuals feel when their gender identity does not align with their biological gender. This can lead to severe depression, eating disorders, self-harm, and even suicide. Leah, a nineteen-year-old transgender college student from Can-

> "When I was born, I was named Matthew. Early on, when I was little, I felt that I wanted to be a girl, but I didn't have a full understanding about it. I knew I was a boy because my mom and dad told me I was one."[3]
>
> —Christina, a trans woman

Gender dysphoria is the distress felt by individuals whose gender identity does not align with their biological gender. This condition can lead to severe depression, self-harm, and suicide.

ada, shares her experience coming to terms with herself and her identity:

Looking back, I had a lot of gender dysphoria starting at a young age—probably 5 or 7, I'd say. I wasn't open about it for a long time. Going through primary and secondary school, I was completely closed off even to my family. It wasn't until shortly after high school when a suicide attempt brought a lot of that to the surface. I was kind of forced to deal with a whole lot more about myself than I usually had. I kind of came out to myself about being transgender.[4]

Sexual Orientation

Sexual orientation is completely separate from gender identity. A person of any gender can identify as straight, bisexual, or gay. When referring to a transgender person's sexual orientation, the orientation relates to the person's gender identity rather than the gender assigned at birth. For example, a transgender woman is a person who was assigned male at birth but identifies as a woman. A straight transgender woman is attracted to men. Recognition of sexual orientation and gender can happen at different times, or it can happen around the same time. Everyone's experience will be different. Jessy, a transgender man, describes his experience at sixteen this way: "I was starting to come to terms with my sexual orientation. I wanted to be a masculine figure in a relationship with a woman, to be seen as a straight man attracted to women."

Quoted in Susan Kuklin, *Beyond Magenta: Transgender Teens Speak Out.* Somerville, MA: Candlewick, 2014, p. 10.

For transgender kids, puberty can be an especially challenging time. Suddenly their bodies are expressing gender in a way completely disconnected from the way they feel and understand their gender. For many it feels like their body is turning against them. This can lead to self-esteem issues and even depression. Amanda, now age forty-five, shares how she experienced puberty: "Like the old clichés, I didn't feel like the other boys. But it was when puberty came when all the wrong signals came up on the screen so to speak. And then all your hormones are racing and that was a troublesome period that started off massive depressions, clinical depressions. Everyone else was having a great time and I was in and out of the hospital with clinical depression."[5]

Today more parents are becoming aware of gender diversity and diverse ways of expressing gender. This means that younger children are gaining access to resources and language that helps and supports them through what can otherwise be a confusing time. Jessy, a transgender college student, shares this story of his father supporting his gender expression at an early age:

> I have preschool pictures of me wearing a suit and a necktie. It was at a Valentine's Day party at school, and you had to dress nice. All the girls at school wore dresses. I said, "Dad, I don't want to wear a dress. Can you pick out a suit and a necktie for me?" And my dad bought a boy's suit and a clip-on necktie. I was about six. I loved wearing suits and neckties. It felt right to me. But usually I wore dresses and stuff.[6]

But even with early support, a person might not yet realize what these feelings mean.

For some transgender people, the realization of who they are may come when they are first exposed to information about transgender people. This was true for Jessy. He knew he did not feel like a girl, but he was not sure what that meant. It was not until he saw something on TV that his identity began to make sense: "When I was sixteen, I saw a TV episode about the transgender community, and the first thing that came into my head was '*Oh, my god!* That could definitely be me!'"[7]

Coming to Terms with One's True Gender

Being transgender comes with many challenges, but perhaps the greatest challenge is coming to terms with one's gender identity. Transgender people usually feel early on that there's something different about them and their relationship to gender. Their gender expression may be slightly different than others, but humans are really good at adapting. It is understandable that if everyone calls someone a boy, the person will begin to act like a boy. However, as that person grows older and more self-aware, there may be a gradual or sudden awakening. Such a realization can be uncomfortable and unsettling.

This is doubly true for older individuals who have spent years living as one gender only to recognize that this is not who they truly are. Such a realization comes with a lot of emotional turmoil, especially when it comes after marriage and childbirth. Elliot Gibson, a trans man who transitioned after age forty, shared this regarding his experience:

> Accepting myself as a man and being ok with the kind of man I am have been the most difficult parts. . . . I'm not a hyper masculine guy, rather I'm ordinary. I'm a guy with a vagina. I'm a guy who knits and crochets. I'm a guy who doesn't care about sports. I'm a guy who bore 2 kids. I used to believe I was a woman with these qualities but found out I am a man. Being a man is just one facet of my identity—all the rest still stands.[8]

Gender is something most people take for granted. So when biology and identity do not align, it can take a long time to recognize what is happening. Once realization dawns, coming to terms with this can be difficult, and the prospect of opening up to other people—or coming out—can be intensely frightening. Not coming out means living with the discomfort of acting as a gender with which one does not identify, whereas coming out involves the risk of rejection, harassment, possibly even bodily harm.

Deciding to Come Out

Surveys have found that transgender people are at a higher risk of unemployment, homelessness, abuse, and violence than the general population. These are very real risks that people must consider when deciding whether to come out as transgender. For adults, coming out at work could mean facing a hostile work environment or even loss of employment. For children in schools, coming out could mean teasing or even bullying. There may also be a battle with school administration to require staff to use the appropriate gender pronoun or to allow access to the bathroom that corresponds with the student's gender identity.

In 2013 Tru Wilson of Vancouver, Canada, transitioned at age ten. Because she transitioned during the summer, her struggles began when she returned to her semiprivate school in the fall. The school would not let her use the girl's bathroom, nor would they refer to her by her correct name or pronouns. She explains that she had fully transitioned. "I had transitioned at home, in sports, at my dance school, everything. There was just one target left, school. . . . My parents already knew it wasn't going to be easy. And they were right. The school wouldn't budge." The family even presented the school with letters from doctors who agreed with Wilson's decision to transition. This had no effect. She continues, "They started recommending their own doctors to give me assessments. Soon my parents realized that they weren't going to get anywhere with the school, and we left."[9]

Wilson's story shows the struggle that young people in this position may face when they attempt to be open about who they are. If Wilson's parents had consented to her being assessed by the school's doctors, it is likely she would have been referred to a therapist whose goal would have been to change her view of herself. She was fortunate to have parents who were prepared to fight for their daughter to be treated with respect and accepted for who she is. Wilson ended up transferring to a different school.

Eventually, she and her parents filed a human rights complaint against the school district. She is proud of the result. She says, "We were able to get a policy made that allows all children to use their preferred bathrooms, uniforms, names, and pronouns. Believe me, it's not a perfect policy, but at least it's a start."[10] Wilson, now seventeen, is a human rights activist and a frequent guest speaker. In 2015 she was named one of Vancouver's fifty most powerful and influential people.

Reaction from Family Members

Another challenge individuals face is that their families may also lack knowledge and understanding of what being transgender means. Just a lack of familiarity and interactions with transgender people can lead to awkwardness. One young trans woman, who came out to her family about a year before being interviewed for a news story about the process, shares, "It's still awkward with my siblings. They don't like to talk or really acknowledge it. I wouldn't say they aren't supportive of LGBT people, but I don't think they've had any contact with trans people before me. The lack of communication might have a lot to do with me being different now than I was a year ago, more than being uncomfortable with transgender people."[11]

Sometimes instead of awkwardness, transgender people may experience hostility or even violence from family members. This is what Nat experienced when learning to express their identity. Nat, who is intersex, uses gender-neutral pronouns such as *their*, *they*, and *them*. The term *intersex* refers to someone who was born with both male and female sex traits. Nat was labeled female at birth, but medical tests as a teen showed that Nat was both sexes. People like Nat are not the only ones who prefer gender-neutral pronouns. Many of those who identify as nonbinary, genderqueer, and gender neutral also use these pronouns when referring to themselves. The meanings of terms like *nonbinary*, *genderqueer*, and *gender neutral* can vary, but basically these refer to people who feel they fall somewhere between male and female, or outside of the male-female binary altogether.

Nat's family, especially their brother, had a really hard time accepting Nat's gender. The year after Nat graduated from high school and started college, things escalated with their brother, ultimately leading to Nat's decision to leave home. Nat shares:

On New Year's Day, my brother started throwing stuff at me. I told him to stop, and he wouldn't. We physically fought. My mom tried to separate us. He was yelling that he wasn't the one with the problem. "*She's* the one with the problem. *She's* the one that ruined the family because *she's* a freak." . . . He said a lot of crap and called me hurtful things like faggot. . . . I needed to get out of the environment that was making me feel bad about myself. I decided to live on my own.[12]

Lack of Medical and Mental Health Resources

A big barrier faced by newly identifying transgender people is the lack of mental health resources. Coming to terms with one's gender identity can be stressful on its own. Add to this the reactions of family members and how expressing one's true gender may impact school, work, and other public situations, and it is easy to see why many transgender individuals seek counseling or psychiatric services. Many may

Many transgender individuals seek counseling to help them come to terms with their gender identity and with reactions from people they know when they decide to come out or transition.

begin their journey toward transitioning by talking to a therapist, but therapists are not required to undergo any training specific to gender diversity. In fact, roughly 20 percent of those who turn to therapists for help coming to terms with their gender identity report being referred to conversion therapy, or therapy that is intended to make individuals identify as the gender they were assigned at birth. Even if the therapist has good intentions, a lack of understanding can result in inadequate care or even cause harm.

Gaining access to gender-affirming medical care can also be a struggle, depending on where one lives and what options are available in that area. Many transgender people seek resources

Conversion Therapy

Sometimes transgender individuals might not feel free to express the gender they identify with. They may be unable or unwilling to transition because of beliefs about what it means to be transgender. For example, they may be part of a religion that does not accept gender diversity. Or they may fear the disapproval of parents or other family members. All of these factors may lead individuals to pursue conversion therapy, sometimes called reparative therapy, either on their own or because of pressure from family members.

Conversion therapy is highly controversial. It is used in an effort to get LGBTQ individuals to be heterosexual or to identify with their biological sex. Recent studies have shown that conversion therapy leads to an increased rate of suicide attempts. A 2019 study found that transgender people who have gone through conversion therapy are twice as likely as other transgender individuals to attempt suicide. This same study showed alarming statistics for transgender children. In the study, transgender children under age ten who underwent conversion therapy were four times more likely to attempt suicide than were members of the general transgender population. Studies such as this, along with personal anecdotes of the damage done by this therapy, have led to bans in some states. Currently, fourteen states and the District of Columbia have passed laws to protect LGBTQ youths from having to undergo conversion therapy.

and medical referrals through local LGBTQ organizations, where such organizations are available. However, there are many places in the United States that lack resources tailored to LGBTQ people. This may lead to some people relocating in order to access the medical care that they need. For many individuals, living as one's true gender is worth all of the sacrifices and hardships that come with it.

Gender is more of a spectrum than a binary system of only male and female. While most people can be found near the ends of this spectrum, there are also people who fall in the middle. It can take time for people to find out where on the gender spectrum they fall. Once they understand their own gender, they may face additional challenges as they come out to their family and consider transitioning in a sometimes unaccepting world.

Chapter Two

Nature, Nurture, or Psychological Condition?

People have long debated the reason behind gender diversity. There are three schools of thought regarding gender diversity. One is that it is a psychological condition. Another is that gender diversity is the result of the environment in which individuals grow up and is nurtured from childhood to adulthood. The third school of thought is that gender diversity is a naturally occurring phenomenon, making it both a natural and normal variation.

Psychological Condition

For most of the 1900s, gender diversity was viewed as a psychological disorder. People who were transgender were treated as if they had a mental illness. When gender-affirmation surgery became available, usually referred to as a sex-change operation, doctors and psychologists acted as gatekeepers. Only those who showed clear signs of living in distress were granted access to surgery or hormone therapy. As a result, transgender people quickly learned to give the answers needed to get past these gatekeepers. Because of this, the medical and psychological communities had huge gaps in knowledge regarding gender diversity, which further perpetuated the view that these were disturbed individuals.

Today transgender people still struggle with the perception that they have a mental disorder. Before 2013 the handbook used by health professionals for diagnosing mental disorders listed a mental illness called gender identity disorder. That changed in 2013. The fifth edition of the *Diagnostic and Statistical Manual of Mental Disorders* dropped gender identity disorder as a diagnosis and replaced it with gender dysphoria. While this removed the word *disorder* from the diagnosis, some feel that the stigma of gender diversity being a mental illness remains.

People who view gender diversity as being a result of biology see no need for a diagnosis of any kind, since only illnesses require diagnoses. At the same time, a diagnosis is the modern-day

Christine Jorgensen (pictured) became a celebrity in the 1950s after undergoing what was then called a sex-change operation. At the time, gender diversity was viewed as a psychological disorder.

gatekeeper between transgender people and living a fully transitioned life. In some states a diagnosis is necessary to access hormone therapy or other medical transition options. Many insurance companies require a diagnosis before covering transitional care. And in some states a diagnosis and/or medical transition is required in order to change gender on birth certificates, driver's licenses, and other documents. All of this reinforces the idea that gender identity is a psychological condition.

Nurture

Although the idea of gender diversity as a psychological disorder has been challenged, it is still more accepted today than one of the other possible explanations—that is, the idea that environmental factors, or how a person is reared or nurtured, can influ-

Because of a botched circumcision, David Reimer (pictured) was reared as a girl. The renowned psychologist who advised his parents to do this wrongly believed that how one is reared determines gender identity.

ence gender identity. The nurture idea has mostly been debunked at this point. There are still therapists who will try to "fix" transgender patients on the basis of this outdated belief, but most now recognize that the external environment has little to no bearing on the internal understanding of one's gender.

There are, however, many members of society who still accept this idea. These include parents, who may be reluctant to allow children to play with toys perceived to be for the other gender. It also includes some religious leaders, who still teach that being LGBTQ is a choice. People with this mind-set will sometimes try to set the transgender child up with a mentor to show them how to be a manly man or a feminine woman in hopes of getting the child to conform with the gender they were assigned at birth.

The idea of nurture being a factor in determining gender identity was debunked famously and tragically decades ago. In 1966 baby Bruce Reimer suffered a botched circumcision that severely injured his penis. Psychologist John Money had long wanted to test his theory that nurture was the primary factor in determining one's gender identity. Money advised Bruce's parents to raise him as a girl named Brenda and never tell him the truth. The Reimers made frequent visits to Money, who reinforced their efforts to raise their child as a girl. But from a young age it was clear that Bruce knew that he was a boy, in spite of his parents' best efforts. As an adult he learned the truth and lived his life as David Reimer. He married and had children, but he continued to struggle with depression from the psychological damage his unusual upbringing caused.

Reimer's struggles were compounded by the psychologist's actions. Money's reports, papers, and an eventual book on the experiment misrepresented as a success the efforts to socialize David to be female. It was not until David went public that Money's accounts began to be debunked. However, this still marked a major setback in transgender care. Eventually David lost his struggle with depression and committed suicide. This tragic story is an example of nature versus nurture and shows that gender is an innate trait and not something that is learned.

Nature

Nature, in this context, refers to the idea that gender diversity is a function of biology—that one's gender is essentially determined by a complex combination of biology and chemistry. Some advocates of this theory point to the gender diversity that occurs in nature. Some animal species have both male and female sex characteristics; others are able to change sex characteristics. For several years, scientists have been looking for ways to explain the existence of transgender people through means of biology. Recently a team of scientists in Spain found concrete evidence to support the idea that brain development plays a role in determining gender identity. The research also found a link between the brains of transgender people and the gender they identify with.

The team used brain scans to measure the white matter of four key areas of the brain. These areas show significant differences in male and female brains. Then the team measured scans of those areas in the brains of transgender adults who had received no hormone therapy or medical affirmation treatment. The white matter in the brains of transgender men was the same as in the brains of cisgender men. The white matter in the brains of transgender women was exactly in the middle of that in the brains of cisgender women and cisgender men. This supports the view that gender diversity is a result of biology and not a choice.

Scientists hope that this new knowledge could lead to earlier identification of transgender children. Having this knowledge could help parents and care providers assist children through smoother transitions. Further studies will be needed to track when and how these white matter areas develop in the brain and to track changes in white matter over time. As of now, it is unknown when the white matter takes on these gendered characteristics or whether white matter changes over time.

Intersex Conditions

There are other ways to measure gender diversity. This is especially true in the case of people who are intersex. Human biological sex characteristics include chromosomes, hormone levels,

Sex Variation in the Animal Kingdom

The animal kingdom is filled with sexual variations. Scientific American magazine has noted that female spotted hyenas found in Tanzania have a clitoris that looks and functions like a penis. These hyenas also have a fused labia that forms a scrotum. When they give birth, the cub is born through the penile canal. In Europe the female old-world mole has both ovarian and testicular tissue. In Botswana lionesses have been spotted with manes that are characteristic of male lions.

Marine biologists have also noted diversity in marine mammals. Some striped dolphins, which are found in both the Pacific and Atlantic Oceans, have external female genitals with testes, and internally they have male sex organs. Bowhead whales, which live in Arctic and subarctic waters, have a diverse sexual makeup. Some have both external female parts and internal male parts. Other marine creatures have gender-bending characteristics. For example, clownfish are born as hermaphrodites, having both male and female characteristics, and will eventually turn male. But when the school needs a new leader, a male will turn into a female for that purpose.

genitals, and secondary characteristics such as breast tissue and facial hair. However, these characteristics do not always follow a binary system. While having XX chromosomes indicates a biological female and XY chromosomes indicate a biological male, there are also those born with XXY or XXXY chromosomes. Genitals can have a wide range of sizes and appearances, with or without a variation in chromosomes. Some changes in genital size or appearance can be caused by prenatal hormone imbalances, but sometimes this is just a naturally occurring phenomenon. There are also individuals who may possess the secondary sex characteristics of both genders or of the opposite gender. Those born with these conditions are known as intersex. It is believed that intersex births make up about 1.7 percent of all births in the United States. This is comparable to the number of people who have red hair.

For a long time the existence of intersex people has been largely hidden. Babies born with visible differences in their genitalia were often subjected to surgeries to alter the appearance of the genitals. Often this was done without the knowledge or consent of the parents, as medical professionals assumed they were sparing parents bad news or unnecessary worry. Many intersex people who had surgery as infants were never told about the circumstances of their birth or surgery. In some instances they began to suspect they were somehow different from their peers at an early age. In other instances they had no real awareness of this until adulthood. Dana, a transgender woman who is intersex, shared this when she was asked about her medical past:

Well, it's hard to know. I had a surgical scar and my father at one point mentioned that they thought something was wrong at birth. And it affected my circumcision. So, there are those hints. . . . So, yeah, I knew, I mean I had serious problems and I knew they had to do with my reproductive system. I started bleeding through my penis so hard, that was pretty freaky. I didn't think that happened to most kids my age in my class. So that was the beginning of when I really knew something was wrong. . . . I say I'm intersexed because I have a uterine remnant and I've menstruated already and I have a female gender identity, so that's mixed with my male genitalia and my XY chromosomes, which I assume I have, so that makes me intersexed.[13]

As society has become more aware of intersex conditions, improvements are happening for intersex health. The rates of genital correction surgeries on infants are going down, for example. The existence of intersex people also supports the argument for diverse gender identities being natural. Human biology is the definition of *natural* that many use, but even biology does not support the idea of a gender binary system. Overall there is still a lot to learn about the diverse range of gender experience and expression. As Shannon, who identifies as genderqueer, or nonbinary, says:

> There are slight genetic differences between people whom we consider to be women and those whom we consider to be men. But 99.9% of the DNA between those two sets of humans is exactly the same. Why do we obsess about that 0.1%? It's ridiculous. Plus, thinking that men and women are opposites of each other, in whatever binary way, completely obscures the existence of intersexuality and intersexed people. There are way more than two sexes and way more than two ways to be gendered. It's just too, too bad that we live in a society where we try to force people into boxes (often successfully) based upon what's between their legs.[14]

Gender as a Social Construct

For simplification, gender expression is often referred to as "how people do gender." Much of how people do gender is more societal and cultural than actually related to gender. Often male and female are viewed as opposites, but there is evidence that points toward men and women being more alike than different. One comparison of research describes gender as a mosaic rather than a binary system. For example, men and women have the same hormones but at different levels, and situations can cause changes to those hormone levels. Testosterone levels

"There are slight genetic differences between people whom we consider to be women and those whom we consider to be men. But 99.9% of the DNA between those two sets of humans is exactly the same. Why do we obsess about that 0.1%?"[14]

—Shannon, a genderqueer individual

29

fluctuate according to the time of day, season, mood, and stress levels. In men these levels drop when they are performing a nurturing role like caring for a child.

Another common belief is that on a psychological level men and women are opposites, but the mosaic example holds true here as well. In a study of college students in which the students recorded which highly gendered activities they enjoyed, less than 1 percent liked only masculine or feminine activities, and 55 percent showed a combination of feminine and masculine behaviors. Other gender stereotypes, like men being better at math than women, have also been debunked by research.

Sociologists are beginning to differentiate between doing gender and being gender. A man, for example, may be a man but do gender as a woman by dressing in drag for a performance.

Sociologists are beginning to differentiate between *doing* gender, or gender expression, and *being* gender, or gender identity. Doing gender is the daily act of gender expression associated with gender roles and societal expectations. It is an act of expression within the gender construct. Being gender is an understanding of one's true gender identity. A man, for example, may be a man but do gender as a woman by dressing in drag for a performance. A transgender man may know that he is a man but continue to do gender as a woman because he is not yet ready to socially transition. A woman or trans woman may identify as a woman but not feel inclined to do gender in the way society expects her to. None of the ways these examples do gender impacts how they are being gender, or their gender identity. Gender expression does not equal gender identity, even though it is a common social cue used to help others understand one's gender identity. And a nonbinary person is still nonbinary even if their gender expression appears to be either male or female. Overall societal acceptance of diverse gender expression is becoming more common.

"After months of attempting to assimilate to what the other girls in my grade were doing—and failing miserably—I tried to kill myself."[15]

—Kurtis, a trans man

Often how someone does gender is a way of exploring and figuring out one's gender identity. Kurtis, a now twenty-four-year-old trans man, shares this from his childhood:

I was a tomboy when I was a kid. There is not a single picture of me before junior high where I don't have a short haircut. Whenever we'd go to the salon I'd look through the haircut books and I'd always reach for the boy's book. My mom would tell me I had to pick from the girl's book, so I'd pick the shortest haircut I could find. It was okay to be a tomboy up until the time I hit junior high. . . . I grew my hair out, and I tried to wear makeup and dresses, but I felt wretched about it. After months of attempting to assimilate to what the other girls in my grade were doing—and failing miserably—I tried to kill myself.[15]

Kurtis went from experimenting with gender expression to trying to conform to gender standards and norms. When that did not work, he fell into depression. This can be a common challenge for those unable to express their gender identity.

How people present gender to the outside world is a complex and diverse range of gender expressions. This range of societally

Chemical Exposure and Gender Diversity

Research has found that synthetic estrogen, which has been used in many products, causes changes in sex characteristics. An article from the National Institute of Environmental Health Science notes that once in the body, synthetic estrogen can imitate, block, or trigger natural hormones. When this happens, the result can be the feminization of males, infertility in both males and females, and early breast development in females.

Synthetic estrogen had many uses in earlier decades. During and after World War II, it had widespread use in agriculture to eradicate insects. In the 1940s diethylstilbestrol (DES), another form of synthetic estrogen, was commonly used to prevent miscarriages. DES may affect both sexual orientation and gender identity, as well as lead to demasculinization in males. DES has also been linked to a rare form of cancer.

Other chemicals have been linked to sexual changes. In recent studies, high levels of phthalates in expecting mothers have been linked to the birth of less "masculine" boys with smaller genitalia. Phthalates are chemical compounds found in makeup, detergent, medicines, and other common products. Additionally, mothers who take certain thyroid medicines or diet pills while pregnant are more likely to have daughters who are lesbian.

sanctioned gender expression is constantly changing over time. Acceptable dress, hairstyle, and cosmetics keep evolving for both men and women.

Dangers of Not Being Able to Express One's True Gender

Being in a position in which one cannot live as one's true gender has been shown to have several negative impacts for transgender people. Many have described it as feeling like they are putting on a performance for others. When healthy transition care, such as hormone therapy, is not available, trans people may feel a lack of control over their bodies and lives.

Medical professionals have noted that trans people frequently develop eating disorders, their weight becoming one area of their lives that they can control. Vicky, a trans woman from New Mexico, shares her struggle with eating disorders: "I struggle with eating. I've been in and out of treatment for eating disorders, but I'm just not able to maintain a diet. If my curves aren't in the right places, I don't want to have them at all. I am still fighting to get on hormones, so I'm trying to pass as a woman without any help. When I'm thinner, it's easier to do that."[16]

It has also been noted that trans people often struggle with depression. Luis, a trans man who transitioned during college, shares some of the internal struggle he felt prior to coming out as trans:

> "We can definitely tell how oppressive our society is when we've gotten to this point where there is an entire subset of people who think that suicide is their only way out."[17]
>
> —Luis, a trans man

When I'm in a really deep fit of depression, I take photographs of myself. It's sort of a way to document my depression. I got to one of the darker pictures and thought, do I want to continue to be like this, or do I want to go through the pain of coming out? This pain is greater, I decided. I don't want to be like this anymore. Prior to coming out, I was definitely suicidal. We can definitely tell how oppressive our society is when we've gotten to this point where there is an entire subset of people who think that suicide is their only way out.[17]

Studies have shown that transgender people, especially teens and people of color, are at a higher risk of suicidal thoughts, attempts, and self-injury. It is clear that these populations need more support and services.

Chapter Three

Transition

Not everyone who is gender diverse decides to transition. But many do. Transitioning means making life changes to live as the gender with which a person identifies. These changes can include social changes. This may mean opening up to family, friends, and coworkers about one's gender identity. It can also mean beginning to live openly as that gender. People often transition in one area of their life, such as at home with family, and then expand to other areas such as school or work. For some, transitioning also includes hormone therapy and possibly surgery.

Deciding to transition can be a big deal. Some people recognize their true gender early in life and want to start living as that gender right away. Other people time their transition around specific life events. Changing schools or graduating from high school is one of these events. Others may transition after college or between jobs. Older adults may wait to transition until their kids are grown or until their parents pass away. There are a lot of different factors that people consider when they are contemplating transition. It is a very personal choice, and no two transition experiences are alike.

Family
Some transgender individuals decide to transition socially before pursuing a medical transition. Social transition involves first coming out to family, friends, coworkers, or fellow students and school administrators. The person may

The decision to transition is a very personal choice. Some people wait for a specific life event, such as high school graduation, to begin the process of transitioning.

then adopt the dress and mannerisms of their true gender. Often this comes with a change of names and pronouns. Sometimes it can be hard to get loved ones to accept new names or pronouns, while other times it does not take much effort.

Casper, a trans man in his twenties who lives in England, had a difficult time when he came out to his parents. At first his parents expressed resistance to the idea that Casper was transgender, but after a lengthy discussion came understanding. Casper shared his experience:

I put my stake in the ground and through tears I told them I realised how hard this was for them, but this was really what I was and if I did not do this they might lose me altogether. Eventually, they seemed to understand to a certain degree. I know I'm lucky, I know many people, some kids just fourteen or fifteen, have at this point being picked up by the scruff of their neck and thrown out of the front door. It was the most emotionally draining conversation of my entire life, but I was glad to come out of it assured of the parental love and domestic/financial support I needed to make it through the road ahead.[18]

Names and Pronouns

Figuring out what to call oneself (and what pronouns other people should use) can be complicated and confusing even when people are trying to do the right thing. J, a nonbinary transgender person who lives in Vermont, shares their experiences at work:

> "It was the most emotionally draining conversation of my entire life, but I was glad to come out of it assured of the parental love and domestic/financial support I needed to make it through the road ahead."[18]
>
> —Casper, a trans man from England

> I regularly introduce myself in meetings with they/them pronouns, talk frequently about being nonbinary, and communicate often about how painful, frustrating, and distracting it is to be misgendered. . . . I can't remember a single work week that I've gone without being misgendered at least once; it often happens multiple times. It is utterly exhausting to be constantly misread and misgendered, to be subjected to my coworkers' incorrect perception of my gender even after I've been so clear about my gender and pronouns with them. I believe that using the right name, pronouns, and language in the workplace shows an investment in connections and relationships. When folks just can't seem to get it right, I doubt their investment.[19]

Sometimes transitioning can cause conflict at work or school. Because there are no federal protections for transgender people, and because state laws vary so much, transitioning can put people into very vulnerable situations. But not all such experiences are bad. Some transitioning individuals have been pleasantly surprised at the reaction from employers and coworkers.

Natalie, a trans woman who works as a police officer in a rural town, shares what she experienced when she transitioned and came out to her boss:

I wore women's clothing at home, and my family had started using my preferred name and pronouns, but as soon as I left the house I had to be a man again. I was so excited to finally get to start being myself full time. When my beard was virtually gone, I started taking a higher dose of estrogen, which led to more and more physical changes. I knew I was running out of time to come out at work. Transitioning on the job is not an easy thing to do but even less so when you're a police officer in a small town. There was only so long I could manage to avoid the locker room, and if I went in, someone would be bound to notice a few things.[20]

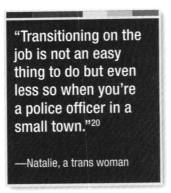

"Transitioning on the job is not an easy thing to do but even less so when you're a police officer in a small town."[20]

—Natalie, a trans woman

Natalie asked to speak with the police chief to explain her situation. She had been looking for jobs in case things did not go well. She says she was shocked when he said, "You know, I've got an aunt who used to be my uncle. I don't give a shit if you're a man or a woman. As long as you do your damn job, it doesn't matter to me which uniform you wear." He agreed to call a meeting to explain the situation to the other employees, and then added,

"If anyone gives you any grief, you just have them take it up with me." I was in a euphoric daze as I stood up. I thanked him over and over again, and I had just reached the door of his office when he called out, "What's your name going to be?" I told him that I was going to change it to Natalie after surgery. He nodded and said, "Great. I'll order you a new badge." I broke into tears the second I left the station.[21]

Unexpected Challenges

Every experience with transitioning will be different. Race, socio-economic status, and assigned gender will all factor into what the transition is like. But there are also some common experiences. One of these involves passing as the gender a person transitions to. This is a challenge mostly faced by those who transition after puberty. Trans women may face more difficulties passing as female without cosmetic surgery. Male puberty leaves trans women with deeper voices, wider shoulders, larger hands, and more hair.

Another challenge that comes with social transition is clothing. It can be expensive to change an entire wardrobe. Erik, a trans man who transitioned as a college student in Idaho, shared the experience of sorting through his clothing:

> There are so many elements to gender that most people never stop to think about. Trans people think about these things constantly. After I came out as trans, I realized I was going to need to update my wardrobe. I gave my cute little skirts and frilly shirts to my sister and slowly began replacing everything in my closet with men's clothes. Some of the items I had I was able to hang on to, but it's amazing how gendered clothing really is.[22]

Hormonal Transition

Some transgender people find that hormone treatment can aid their transition. Hormone therapy causes physical changes that can help transgender people feel more like their true gender. Not all transgender people opt for hormone therapy. Like all parts of a person's transition, this is a very individualized choice. Some transgender children who come out to their families and have family support begin taking hormonal supplements to delay the onset of puberty. This

"After I came out as trans, I realized I was going to need to update my wardrobe . . . Some of the items I had I was able to hang on to, but it's amazing how gendered clothing really is."[22]

—Erik, a trans man

can make transitioning and passing as their true gender a little easier. Kelly, a transgender woman attending college in Iowa, came out as transgender at age twelve. She shares her experience with using hormones before puberty, commonly called puberty blockers:

> I am one of those extremely lucky people who came out before I started puberty. My moms pushed really hard for me to be able to take puberty-suppressing hormones. Basically, hormone blockers just give trans youth a medication that tells your body to press pause on puberty. Once you've met the other therapy requirements, you can start taking estrogen or testosterone and go through puberty as your desired sex rather than your biological sex.[23]

Male-to-Female Hormone Treatment

Hormone therapy for individuals who wish to transition from male to female is used to suppress the male hormone testosterone. Testosterone is the most powerful of the male hormones, leading to an increased sex drive, male-pattern baldness, and facial hair. An androgen suppressant is used to lessen the amount of testosterone impacting the body. After that, an estrogen supplement is added. Estrogen is the hormone that is more predominant in women. Trans women who use estrogen usually use it for life, or at least for a long time to achieve the desired effects for transition.

Estrogen causes many physical changes. These changes are similar to what girls experience when starting puberty. During the first few years on estrogen, breast tissue will increase steadily, although trans women will not develop large breasts from estrogen usage. Body hair may decrease with the use of estrogen, but facial hair can be resistant to the effects of estrogen. To get rid of unwanted facial hair, many trans women use the costly laser hair

Transitioning Can Ease Gender Dysphoria

Gender dysphoria is the discomfort of one's gender identity and one's physical body not aligning. This discomfort can become very severe, leading to depression, self-harm, or suicidal thoughts or actions. Even when not that severe, it can be very distressing. Delaying transitional care can make these feelings worse. Social transition, hormone therapy, and gender-affirming surgeries can ease this discomfort as a person's life becomes more in line with their gender identity.

Jackson, a transgender man from Texas, had not yet transitioned when he experienced intense feelings while dressing for a formal event that he planned to attend. He describes his distress:

> From the second I put on my standard little black dress alone in my hotel room, something felt off. I couldn't flip the switch. I was looking in the mirror and all I could see was an ugly, mannish person in a dress . . . for me, staring at myself in the mirror, all I could see was wrong, wrong, wrong. I hadn't felt this prickling full-body discomfort, inside and out, since I was a little kid clawing at my parents in desperation as they pulled a dress over my head.

Jackson Bird, *Sorted: Growing Up, Coming Out, and Finding My Place (A Transgender Memoir)*. New York: Tiller, 2019.

removal technique known as electrolysis. Estrogen also prevents baldness, but for trans women who have already experienced some hair loss, it may not regrow.

The side effects of estrogen make it unsuitable as a treatment for male baldness in the general population. However, estrogen's many side effects are desirable in trans women who wish to attain more feminine physical features. One side effect of taking estrogen is that it can cause a softening of skin texture to more closely resemble a woman's skin texture. Trans women who take estrogen also experience a decrease in muscle mass and a shift in fat deposits. Instead of a male pattern of fat distribution, with the majority of fat in the belly, the fat will shift to a more female pattern. Fat deposits will develop in the butt, hips, and thighs, creating a curvier and more feminine figure.

The reproductive system also changes with estrogen therapy. Typically, sex drive and sperm production decrease. This can cause a decrease in fertility, which may be irreversible.

Another side effect of estrogen is that it can lead to emotional changes. Some trans women may become easily upset or emotional. Others just find it easier to express their feelings. Hormone therapy often enables trans women to feel more complete and more like their true gender.

Some things do not change with the use of estrogen. Vocal ranges and pitch will stay the same in trans women. Many trans women seek out speech coaches or take voice lessons in order to learn and practice a more feminine tone.

Laser hair removal, a costly procedure, helps many trans women get rid of unwanted facial hair.

Female-to-Male Hormone Treatment

For female-to-male transition, the male hormone testosterone is used. The goal with testosterone (or T, as trans men typically call it) is to get hormone levels on par with a biological male. Testosterone is given through an injection every two weeks either for life or until the desired effects have been achieved. The changes that trans men experience when starting testosterone are similar to those experienced by a boy entering puberty.

One of the most notable effects for trans men taking testosterone is that menstruation ceases. Those who continue to have a monthly period after about six months usually adjust testosterone levels until menstruation stops.

Testosterone leads to a variety of other changes. Trans men on testosterone may go bald, similar to what many men experience. They will also experience an increase in body and facial hair. It can take years of being on testosterone to achieve the facial hair coverage a trans man may desire. These changes in facial and body hair are some of the reasons trans men on testosterone are able to pass as biologically male in day-to-day interactions. Quinn, a trans man who lives in Portland, Maine, shares the following about his experience growing body hair while on testosterone: "Most people get tired of me talking about my body hair within the first five minutes, but my girlfriend has been great about it. She will listen to me talk about how patchy my leg hair is, or how my right leg is hairier than my left leg. . . . She will scratch my back for me because I have so many hairs sprouting up and it's so itchy."[24]

Another change that comes with testosterone is the lowering in pitch of the voice. Unlike for trans women on estrogen, trans men on testosterone will be able to achieve the vocal range of their true gender with hormone therapy.

Sexual changes occur for trans men as well. Testosterone can contribute to a higher sex drive. It can also cause the clitoris to become enlarged.

Testosterone also changes skin texture. A trans man's skin becomes more coarse. Acne and oily skin are other side effects of testosterone, but these usually only occur at the beginning of treatment.

Trans men will experience a change in body fat distribution, with fat shifting to the abdomen. Hips, butts, and thighs will become leaner. Muscle mass also increases, which results in overall weight gain. The end result of these changes is a more masculine body appearance.

Emotional changes also occur. Like trans women, trans men often feel more like their true selves when on hormone therapy. Testosterone may also make it harder to express certain emotions, and actions like crying may be more difficult.

Gender Policing

As people transition, especially when using hormone therapy to transition, there can be a period of time when they do not fit neatly inside gender expectations. This period of time can be dangerous and can put the transgender person at risk of violence. Even when violence does not occur, awkward and uncomfortable situations can take place. This is especially true when others try to police gender behavior and gendered spaces. This struggle becomes most pronounced in the everyday act of using a public bathroom. Raven, a trans man, shares his experience trying to use a public bathroom shortly after beginning hormone therapy:

> While transitioning, I go to the bathroom in a movie theater. The female ticket taker objects when I try to go into the ladies' room. The male ticket taker objects when I try to go into the men's room. When I confront them both and ask which I should use, they refuse to come up with an answer, both just desperately reiterating that I can't go in either "for the sake of the other patrons." Rather than call the manager, make a scene, and leave my kid sitting for a long time alone in the theater, I go out back and piss in a dumpster and then went back to the film.

Quoted in Lori B. Girshick, *Transgender Voices: Beyond Women and Men*. Hanover, NH: University Press of New England, 2008, p. 133.

Surgical Transitions

Not all transgender people can achieve all the physical changes they want from hormones alone. For example, for trans men testosterone does not cause a decrease in breast tissue. For trans men to achieve a desired flat-chested appearance, other methods must be used. For many trans men, this means binding, or wrapping the chest tightly to hide breast tissue. This can be extremely uncomfortable and can lead to long-term problems with breathing and back pain. Top surgery, or breast reduction surgery, is another option trans men may pursue. There are other surgical options available for both trans men and trans women.

Surgical transition has been referred to as many different things. For a long time it was called sex change surgery or sex reassignment surgery, but many felt that this did not accurately reflect what transgender people were trying to achieve. It was not a reassignment; it was an attempt to bring the external and the internal into alignment to reflect the person's true gender. To better represent the goal of these surgeries, they are now most often referred to as gender-affirming surgeries.

There are many different surgical options available for both trans men and trans women. Like all parts of a person's transition, the choices of which surgeries to pursue, or if any should be pursued, is a very individual decision. Some trans people are happy with their transition without having any surgeries, while others want to achieve a body that most closely matches their true gender through multiple surgeries. Russ, who identifies as transmasculine and uses gender-neutral pronouns, shares their feelings about not using surgical options for their transition:

> I think one of the reasons I'm not pressing a hormonal intervention is because I'm so comfortable with my body. I can look at myself naked and not have a problem with it ... At this point I don't know if I have more of a preference

for feminine or masculine pronouns, so I typically go by gender neutral. I may still transition someday, but I don't want to rush into anything unless I'm absolutely sure. I'm pretty laid back about it.[25]

Cost is another major factor that influences people's decisions regarding surgery. Insurance rarely covers the cost of gender-affirming surgery. Many people may have fewer surgeries than they would have wished because of the cost associated with it. The cost can range anywhere from $100 for a single electrolysis visit to $10,000 for top surgery such as breast augmentation to over $25,000 for bottom surgery, or genital reconstruction. In a study cited in *Translational Andrology and Urology*, about 25 percent of transgender people have had at least one gender-affirming surgery in spite of the high cost.

Male-to-Female Surgeries

Trans women often experience breast growth when on the hormone estrogen, but it may not be as much as they would hope. In order to achieve a more developed chest, some trans women undergo breast augmentation surgery, or mammoplasty. This procedure is similar to the breast enlargement surgery that is available to nontrans women.

Genital surgery may also be performed. For trans women, this often means a vaginoplasty, which is a procedure that creates a vagina out of a penis.

Trans women may also have plastic surgery performed to achieve a more feminine face. There are several different procedures that can be done to feminize the face. Recontouring the forehead so that the brow is higher and the distance between the brow and the hairline is shorter is one. Reshaping the nose to be smaller and more feminine is another. Chins are also often reshaped, sometimes along with the jaw line. Some trans women also have cheek implants. Many trans women will also have their Adam's apple, the protruding part of the male trachea, surgically shaved to be less noticeable.

Female-to-Male Surgeries

To avoid the need to bind, many trans men have chest, or top, surgery. There are a couple of different ways to do this, but one is a double mastectomy that removes both breasts. Sometimes this is followed by a nipple graft, which reshapes and resizes the nipples to achieve the look of a male chest. Mastectomies and nipple grafts are considered major surgeries, but many people are able to recover at home without a hospital stay.

It is less common for trans men to have bottom surgery, or lower surgery, but some go this route. There are several surgical options, but the two most common are metoidioplasty and phalloplasty. Both of these surgeries attempt to construct a penis. However, these procedures have varying levels of success, and the results rarely have the level of sensation desired.

Additionally, many trans men will have a hysterectomy preformed, which is the removal of the uterus. When having this procedure done, trans men may also have the cervix, fallopian tubes, and

A surgical team performs a hysterectomy. Many trans men undergo this uterus removal because their female anatomy feels foreign to them.

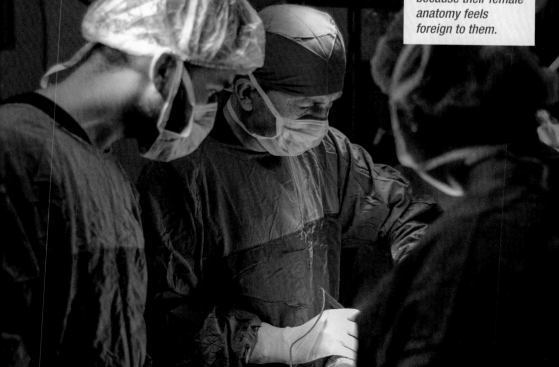

ovaries removed as well. Having these reproductive organs removed can have several benefits for trans men. Some trans men want them removed simply because these parts feel foreign to them. Another benefit is that this eliminates the need for gynecological visits, which can be very uncomfortable for trans men. Having the ovaries removed also means a person will be exposed to less estrogen, which can be very desirable to trans men.

The goal of each method of transition is to help trans individuals live life more fully as the gender they identify as. Transitioning to living as one's true gender has many mental health benefits. For some trans people, a social transition is all that is needed for them to feel like their true selves. For others, hormones may help them reach their desired transition. And for some, surgery is needed. Transitioning is an individual journey—and it will be different for every transgender person.

Chapter Four

The Struggle for Trans Rights

Since beginning to gain public recognition in Western culture in the 1950s, trans people have struggled to have their identities publicly recognized, and to enjoy the same human rights as other people. In many cases this includes protesting acts of violence against transgender people. The past few decades have been marked by huge leaps forward and some steps backward.

Violence

The FBI began tracking gender identity–related hate crimes in 2013. While the agency's tracking system is imperfect, it at least provides a snapshot of hate-motivated violence in the United States. In 2018, of the 7,120 hate crimes recorded by the FBI, nearly 19 percent targeted people who identify as LGBTQ. Most of these victims were gay men, but a large number were transgender. Out of all reported hate crimes for 2018, 168 victims were targeted because they were transgender or gender nonconforming. This makes up approximately 2.4 percent of reported hate crimes. While this number may not seem large, it represents a 34 percent rise in anti-trans violence from 2017, and includes at least twenty-two murders of transgender people.

And while the FBI does track hate crimes that occur because of gender identity, the majority of states do not yet classify gender identity–based attacks as hate crimes. The FBI relies on reports from state agencies to track hate crimes, and in 2018, 80 percent of agencies reported that no hate crimes occurred in their jurisdictions. If states are not considering gender identity as a basis of a hate crime, then there are potentially many hate crimes going unreported. Another concern is that not all victims of hate crimes report the crime to the police. While the methods used to track crimes are imperfect, such a large rise in crimes victimizing transgender people is cause for concern.

The transgender community is working to make these statistics more visible. Every year on November 20, transgender individuals and their allies gather to honor and remember transgender people who have died. The first Transgender Day of Remembrance took place in 2000 to honor the memory of Rita Hester, a trans woman who was murdered the previous year. Similar gatherings have taken place around the country every year since then. Aside from honor-

Photographs of transgender people killed by violence are displayed at a Transgender Day of Remembrance gathering. This annual event raises awareness about ongoing violence against transgender individuals.

ing those who have died, it is a time to highlight concerns about the ongoing violence directed at transgender people. Olivia, a trans woman who lives in North Carolina, shares the following about the Transgender Day of Remembrance: "The biggest celebration in the transgender community is Trans Day of Remembrance, where we hold vigils to memorialize our dead. The rates of suicide, murder, and drug overdose in the trans community are astronomically high. People in all parts of the world gather each November with pictures of our trans loved ones. We celebrate their lives and mourn their deaths."[26]

Bathroom Bills

Some of the violence that transgender people face is over everyday acts that most people take for granted. Using a public restroom is something most people do not think twice about, but it can put transgender people at risk. Because of the risk of violence associated with others' perception that they are using the wrong restroom, many transgender people try to avoid using public restrooms. Not using the bathroom for long periods of time poses many health risks, including urinary tract infections.

To further complicate the bathroom issues, some people support legislation that makes it illegal for transgender people to use the bathroom of the gender they identify with. The United States has experienced a vast wave of bathroom bills in recent years. The bathroom debate began in earnest in 2013. That year the Colorado Civil Rights Division ruled in favor of Coy Mathis, a six-year-old transgender child, allowing her to use the girl's bathroom at her elementary school.

Following this ruling, many conservative lawmakers put forth bills that would require transgender people to use the bathroom that corresponds with their biological gender. As of 2017 there were sixteen states with proposed bathroom bills. In February

2017 North Carolina became the first state to pass a bathroom bill into law, one of the most restrictive that prevented transgender people from using public restrooms of the gender they identify with. This was followed by protests and the state being boycotted by high-profile performers like Bruce Springsteen and sporting organizations like the National Collegiate Athletic Association. The bill was repealed in March 2017.

The tide began to shift in 2018, with legislation in Vermont, Hawaii, and New Jersey all leading to more inclusive policies in those states. In 2019, only one state—Indiana—attempted to prevent transgender people from using the restrooms of the gender they

Bruce Springsteen (pictured) joined other celebrities in boycotting North Carolina after legislators passed a law that prevented transgender people from using public restrooms of the gender they identify with.

identify with. Efforts in seven other states were focused on protecting the rights of transgender people to use those restrooms.

Kelly, a trans woman in college who transitioned at age twelve, lobbies for more inclusive school policies. In some schools, trans students have been told to use staff bathrooms. Although this solution might be well-intended, it often leads to more problems for trans students. She explains, "There have been countless cases where trans or disabled students have been told that they can only use the staff bathroom, and this isolates them from the other kids. For trans students who may be stealth, this is a big red flag to their peers. Why do you get to use that bathroom? You're not disabled, so what's wrong with you? It's not a legitimate solution.[27]

Other Issues in Education

In addition to bathroom struggles, transgender students face other forms of discrimination in education. This usually involves rules regarding uniforms, struggles with administration over changing names and gender pronouns, the use of locker rooms, and participation on sports teams that align with one's gender identity. In the case of all-girls or all-boys schools, being admitted to the school that aligns with one's gender identity can be a problem. Kelly notes these issues revolve around the same types of questions as in the bathroom debates. She says, "These same issues crop up in gym class. Which locker room do trans students use? What about if they try out for sports? Will they be allowed?"[28]

While public K–12 schools remain at the forefront of these debates, there have been controversies at the college level as well. Recently in the United States, all women's colleges have been lobbied to change policies to allow the admission of transgender women. This began with Smith College in 2013, when school officials denied admission to Calliope Wong, a transgender woman. Student activists rallied over the incident, engaging the college administration in a long, drawn-out battle over allowing the admission of all individuals who identify as women. In 2014 Mills

College became the first women's college to open admissions to transgender women. Later that same year, Mount Holyoke College did the same. Most women's colleges began making changes following the actions taken at Mills College and Mount Holyoke College. The last women's colleges to change their admissions policy to include transgender women were Smith College and Barnard College, which both began admitting trans women in 2015. Most of the policy change efforts at these colleges were led by student activists.

While there are no federal laws specific to protecting transgender people in education, there is one federal law that is being interpreted to include protections for transgender people. The federal law, Title IX, was passed in 1972 and protects individuals from sex-based discrimination in schools. Originally meant to protect women and girls, multiple courts have ruled that this law includes protection from discrimination based on gender identity. This provides many different protections for transgender people, mostly related to being treated as the gender they identify as. This protection comes regardless of where they are in their transition or whether they have changed their gender on official paperwork. This includes usage of preferred names and pronouns, protection from bullying and harassment, the right to use bathrooms, and a right to privacy. School officials cannot out a transgender student. Schools cannot bar transgender students from school activities. They must afford transgender students with the same educational and student life opportunities as any other student.

Employment

School is not the only place where transgender people face discrimination. Employment continues to be a struggle. One early study revealed that transgender people were unemployed at twice the rate of other Americans. Much like with education, there are gaps in protection for transgender people in the workforce. While there are federal laws and state laws against sex-based discrimi-

Religious Experiences

Not all religions are welcoming of transgender people. Many outright reject trans individuals, while others may put harsh or unreasonable restrictions on their faith membership and participation. However, there are exceptions; a few religions have embraced their transgender members.

This has been the case for Kori Pacyniak, a nonbinary priest. Pacyniak knew as a young child that they wanted to be a priest, but they were assigned female at birth, and their strict Catholic family told them that being a priest was not an option. Determined to pursue a religious life, Pacyniak studied theology in college. They originally transitioned to male but quickly realized that this was not their identity. Pacyniak also struggled with their faith. They searched for a church that was similar to Catholicism and also accepting of Pacyniak's nonbinary identity.

While learning to minister to LGBTQ service members in a postgraduate program, Pacyniak heard that San Diego's Mary Magdalene Apostle Catholic Community was looking for a pastor. Mary Magdalene grew out of a Catholic ordination of women movement, which pushed for priesthood for women. The church is not recognized by the Catholic Church. Even so, Pacyniak has been embraced by this religious community and has realized their childhood dream of being a priest.

nation in the workplace, there are no laws specific to LGBTQ people. However, many of the laws against sex-based discrimination have been interpreted by courts to include gender expression and gender identity.

These rights include the right not to be fired or denied a job or promotion because of gender identity, the right to use the bathroom that aligns with one's gender identity, and the right to a work environment free of sex-based harassment. Sex-based harassment is illegal, and this includes jokes about transgender people, repeatedly using the wrong names or pronouns, and probing personal questions.

In 2017 Attorney General Jeff Sessions issued a memo stating that the US Department of Justice would no longer pursue civil court cases involving discrimination against transgender people. However, attempts by the attorney general and the Trump administration to ignore the law does not change the law, nor does it undo the past two decades of court rulings, which have largely been in favor of the rights of transgender people in the workplace.

In 2020 the Supreme Court was considering a case that could determine whether Title VII of the Civil Rights Act (which protects against discrimination on the basis of sex) also protects transgender people in the workplace. Oral arguments for the case were heard in October 2019. The case, *R.G. & G.R. Harris Funeral Homes Inc. v. Equal Employment Opportunity Commission*, involves Aimee Stephens, who had worked as a funeral director for Harris Funeral Homes for six years as a man. When she came out as transgender and began transitioning to living as a woman, she was fired.

Several state and federal cases have already extended Title VII protections to transgender people. Despite these protections, transgender people can still be forced out of jobs when the work environment becomes hostile. This was the experience of Owen, a transgender man who was working as a mechanic in Alabama. "I floated the idea of transitioning by my supervisor once," he says, "and the response was not good. He told me that he wouldn't let freaks work in his garage, and shortly thereafter all of the other employees started to become increasingly hostile toward me. I quit a few weeks later."[29]

Owen relocated to Boston, hoping for a less hostile environment to transition in. He struggled to find a mechanic job as a woman before his transition. He knew that finding a new job and then transitioning could once again make him unemployed. He continues his story:

> I started taking testosterone, and after a few months my voice had lowered substantially. Some customers still called me she, but most of them referred to me as a guy.

Since I was being seen as male more often than female, I figured it was time to change my name. A month later, I was put on suspension at work. Too many of the other guys complained about working with me, so they were looking for any reason to fire me. I quit before they had the opportunity. I work at a different garage now. When I applied for the job, I said that I was male on the application form. At this point, I pass really well, so they don't know the difference. I'm stealth at work, but I have to be really careful that no one ever finds out that I'm not fully a guy, or else I'll be looking for work again.[30]

Health Care

A more dangerous area where transgender people can face discrimination is health care. There are federal and state laws in place that protect transgender people receiving medical care or purchasing health insurance. For instance, under the Affordable Care Act, it is illegal for health insurance companies to deny transitional care. It is also illegal for health insurance companies to cover a service for some patients and not cover the same service for transgender patients. For example, if a health insurance company covers breast reconstruction services for cancer patients or hormone therapy for women receiving postmenopausal treatment, it must also cover those services for patients with gender dysphoria. Insurance companies also cannot deny people coverage, charge them higher rates, or drop them from their plan on the basis of their transgender identity.

"I'm stealth at work, but I have to be really careful that no one ever finds out that I'm not fully a guy, or else I'll be looking for work again."[30]

—Owen, a trans man

Health care providers are also required by the Affordable Care Act to provide the same treatment to all patients regardless of gender identity. Health providers legally mandated to provide fair access to care include doctors, hospitals, nursing homes and rehabilitation facilities, health clinics in schools or colleges, veteran health centers, drug rehabilitation programs, health services in prisons or detention centers, and rape crisis centers. Health care providers cannot refuse to treat people because they are transgender. Providers cannot insist on unnecessary and intrusive examinations. A person's gender identity must be respected when it comes to making room assignments and in bathroom designations. Harassment, or ignoring harassment by others, is also prohibited. Health care providers also cannot require someone to participate in conversion therapy that intends to change one's gender identity.

Despite these laws protecting transgender patients, many still face discrimination when seeking health care. At best this

Travel

Safety and privacy is a concern for transgender people who travel. This is especially true for air travel because of increased security screening. For example, the full-body screening done at the airport can unintentionally out a trans person. Many of the common items trans individuals may wear in order to present as their gender identity, like chest binders or breast forms, may trigger sensors as a safety concern and cause a passenger to require a pat-down. As with any passenger, pat-downs should be performed by someone of the same gender identity.

Traveling with prosthetics or medications that require syringes can also cause additional security concerns. But again, as with other passengers, transgender people can get a letter from their doctor stating that the device or the medication is medically necessary. This should ease the process of going through security.

Transgender passengers may also have concerns when their gender presentation does not match the gender marker on their identification. This should not be an issue, however, when going through security or boarding the plane. The only important thing is that the name and gender marker on the ticket and on the identification match.

comes from providers lacking knowledge. At worst it is intentional discrimination. This intentional discrimination may come from insurance companies refusing to cover gender-affirming services or from providers refusing to treat transgender patients.

Recently the US Department of Health and Human Services contemplated a rule that would allow doctors and insurance companies to deny health services to transgender people on the basis of religious beliefs. While the rule ultimately was rejected, the debate on the rule generated many comments sharing personal experiences with health care discrimination. A transgender woman in Georgia named Stephe Koontz says she was denied care for ordinary medical issues that had nothing to do with being transgender. In at least two instances, she recalls being told "'We don't treat people like you.' I can't tell you how many times I have been denied even making an appointment once they learn I am a transgender woman."[31]

Housing

Housing can pose another challenge for transgender people. According to the National Center for Transgender Equality, one in five transgender people have experienced housing discrimination. And more than one in ten have been evicted once their gender identity was known. Additionally, one in five have experienced homelessness at some point in their lives. Housing discrimination should not be taking place. While there is not a national law that protects transgender people from housing discrimination, there are many laws that do protect transgender people. Transgender people are protected under the federal Fair Housing Act under the section that prohibits discrimination based on sex. This law covers rental property, housing sales, residential service programs, and temporary shelters. US Department of Housing and Urban Development rules also prohibit discrimination based on gender identity in all federally funded housing.

In addition to these federal protections, there are also some state and local protections. Almost every state prohibits sex-based discrimination in housing. Additionally, eighteen states, the District of Columbia, and more than two hundred cities and counties have passed laws that prohibit housing discrimination based on gender identity or sexual orientation.

These laws protect individuals from many things. Transgender people cannot be denied admittance to homeless shelters. Real estate agents, landlords, and rental companies cannot say a property is unavailable for sale or rent when it is. These groups cannot set different requirements or terms for renters or buyers who are transgender. Banks cannot deny loans or set different terms for loans based on a person's gender identity.

In spite of these protections, discrimination still happens. Without a federal law prohibiting discrimination, transgender people are still at risk. Theodore Pavlich, a transgender man in Ohio, a state with no laws protecting transgender people, experienced this firsthand when he moved into an apartment with a roommate. Everything was fine until the roommate learned that Pavlich was transgender. At that point, the roommate began discussions with the landlord, and plans were made to evict Pavlich almost immediately. Pavlich says, "He told me I couldn't live there [in the apartment] because he wanted a 'family friendly household.' I hadn't broken any part of the lease or done anything wrong. I never even met my landlord—he only communicated with me through my roommate."[32]

Military Service

Another place where transgender people face discrimination is in the armed forces. Transgender people make large contributions to the United States in a variety of occupations, including in the armed forces. According to a recent study by the National Center for Transgender Equality, one in five transgender people are service members or veterans. For a long time, transgender individuals were strictly barred from military service in the United

States. In 2016 the Obama administration lifted the ban, allowing transgender people to serve openly in the military. This victory for transgender service members was short lived, however. In July 2017 President Donald Trump announced plans on Twitter to reinstate the ban. Shortly after, he released a presidential memorandum, citing medical cost and disruption as reasons for the ban to be reinstated. Several lawsuits followed, and a back-and-forth battle ensued for many months. In November 2018 the Supreme Court ruled in favor of Trump's ban, which went into effect on January 22, 2019.

Transgender veterans face unique challenges. Most transitioned after completing military service, and so their military records reflect outdated names and gender markers. This can create a barrier to accessing benefits and can also lead to discrimination or harassment when using a military ID that reflects the wrong gender.

Businesses That Serve the Public

Transgender discrimination can impact a person's life in a wide variety of ways, including the most basic everyday transactions, like going to the store. Naomi Wilde, a transgender college student who lives in Virginia, shares the following:

> I always have my hair and makeup perfect to help me pass. I don't think non trans women think about this as much as trans women do. Once I had a bad cold, and it made my face extra puffy. I went to the corner store near my apartment for medicine, I don't usually shop there. And the guy just started yelling at me to get out. It was so embarrassing. Normally I'd say something back, but I was so sick I just left. I don't shop there at all now. When I walk past that store I feel unsafe.[33]

Businesses that are open to the public, legally called public accommodations, like the store in Wilde's story, should be safe and open for all people to use. Public accommodations include public businesses like restaurants, stores, hotels, and so forth. Federal laws prohibit discrimination in public accommodations for race, religion, national origin, and disability, but not for sex or gender identity. However, forty-four states and the District of Columbia prohibit discrimination on the basis of sex in public accommodations. Many courts have interpreted these laws to include gender identity. Additionally, seventeen states have laws that specifically protect transgender people from discrimination in public accommodations.

These various laws protect individuals in several different ways. Under these laws transgender people have the right to enjoy a business's goods and services on an equal basis with oth-

"I went to the corner store near my apartment for medicine, I don't usually shop there. And the guy just started yelling at me to get out. It was so embarrassing."[33]

—Naomi Wilde, a trans woman

ers and cannot be denied goods and services because of gender identity. Transgender people have the right to express their gender identity in public and cannot be turned away because of dress or appearance. The management of the business is also responsible for ensuring that transgender customers are not harassed by employees or other customers.

Wilde's experience illustrates that in spite of these protections, discrimination does still happen. This is true of all areas in which transgender people face unequal treatment. Even though there are laws protecting individuals from harassment, not all people have the time or the energy to pursue legal action. Whether it is being denied service in a restaurant, not being able to find affordable housing, being fired unfairly from a job, or just struggling to find a bathroom, most trans people are focused on getting through life as best they can. Even when someone is willing to seek legal action, it can be hard to prove that discrimination took place. There are many areas in which the civil rights and liberties of transgender people can be better protected.

Source Notes

Introduction: What Is Gender?

1. Mason Martinez, "My Name Is Mason Martinez," *YCteen*, November/December, 2018. www.ycteenmag.org.

Chapter 1: Finding Oneself

2. Quoted in Sally Hines, *TransForming Gender: Transgender Practices of Identity, Intimacy and Care*. Bristol, UK: Policy, 2007, p. 51.
3. Quoted in Susan Kuklin, *Beyond Magenta: Transgender Teens Speak Out*. Somerville, MA: Candlewick, 2014, p. 34.
4. Quoted in German Lopez, "9 Transgender People Talk About When They Knew, Coming Out, and Finding Love," Vox, April 23, 2015. www.vox.com.
5. Quoted in Hines, *TransForming Gender*, p. 53.
6. Quoted in Kuklin, *Beyond Magenta*, p. 4.
7. Quoted in Kuklin, *Beyond Magenta*, p. 10.
8. Elliot Gibson, interview with the author, January 20, 2020.
9. Quoted in Aaron Devor and Ardel Haefele-Thomas, *Transgender*. Santa Barbara, CA: ABC-CLIO, 2019, p. 146.
10. Quoted in Devor and Haefele-Thomas, *Transgender*, p. 146.
11. Quoted in Lopez, "9 Transgender People Talk About When They Knew, Coming Out, and Finding Love."
12. Quoted in Kuklin, *Beyond Magenta*, pp. 143–44.

Chapter 2: Nature, Nurture, or Psychological Condition?

13. Quoted in Lori B. Girshick, *Transgender Voices: Beyond Women and Men*. Hanover, NH: University Press of New England, 2008, p. 30.
14. Quoted in Girshick, *Transgender Voices*, p. 50.
15. Quoted in Jackson Wright Shultz, *Trans/Portraits: Voices from Transgender Communities*. Hanover, NH: Dartmouth College Press, 2015, p. 9.

16. Quoted in Shultz, *Trans/Portraits*, p. 94.
17. Quoted in Shultz, *Trans/Portraits*, p. 96.

Chapter 3: Transition

18. Casper J. Baldwin, *Not Just a Tomboy: A Trans Masculine Memoir*. London: Jessica Kingsley, 2018, p. 185.
19. J River Helms, interview with author, May 3, 2020.
20. Quoted in Shultz, *Trans/Portraits*, pp. 66–67.
21. Quoted in Shultz, *Trans/Portraits*, p. 67.
22. Quoted in Shultz, *Trans/Portraits*, p. 70.
23. Quoted in Shultz, *Trans/Portraits*, p. 45.
24. Quoted in Shultz, *Trans/Portraits*, p. 50.
25. Quoted in Shultz, *Trans/Portraits*, p. 65.

Chapter 4: The Struggle for Trans Rights

26. Quoted in Shultz, *Trans/Portraits*, p. 83.
27. Quoted in Shultz, *Trans/Portraits*, pp. 172.
28. Quoted in Shultz, *Trans/Portraits*, pp. 172.
29. Quoted in Shultz, *Trans/Portraits*, p. 154.
30. Quoted in Shultz, *Trans/Portraits*, p. 154.
31. Quoted in Diana Tourjee, "12 Reasons It Should Be Illegal for Doctors Not to Treat Trans People," *Vice*, www.vice.com.
32. Quoted in Freedom for All Americans, "Ohio Writer and Activist Uses Discrimination Experience in His Fight for Other Transgender People," 2018. www.freedomforallamericans.org.
33. Naomi Wilde, interview with the author, April 2, 2020.

Ways to Support Transgender Friends and Family

When people learn that someone close to them is coming out as transgender, the most helpful reaction is to show love and support. Here are some basic ways to do that:

1. Use the correct pronouns and names. This can be challenging when a person is used to referring to someone by a different name and pronouns, but it shows a great deal of respect to use the name and pronouns that have been requested. Gender-neutral pronouns can be particularly challenging, but practice helps.

2. Help others use correct pronouns and names. This could mean providing gentle correction on occasion.

3. Do not ask prying questions. If the trans person volunteers information, that is one thing. But it is best not to ask prying questions about the person's body, medical interventions, and other personal topics.

4. When interacting with new people, do not assume that you know someone's gender. It may be easy to see how they present gender, but in the cases of nonbinary individuals, appearances can be deceiving. When possible, avoid using gendered language.

5. Be prepared to deal with people who are resistant to gender-neutral language and practices. Although society is becoming more aware of gender diversity and there are more gender-neutral practices being used, there are those who are resistant to these changes.

DC Center

www.thedccenter.org

Based in Washington, DC, the DC Center is dedicated to providing support for LGBTQ people through promoting community building, health and wellness, arts and culture, and social support. The center's website has a lot of transgender and gender-queer resources and activities.

GLAAD

www.glaad.org

Founded in 1985, GLAAD seeks to rewrite perceptions of the LGBTQ community through the usage of media. GLAAD highlights news stories and entertainment news that promotes a positive view of LGBTQ people, including transgender people.

Human Rights Campaign

www.hrc.org

Founded in 1980, the Human Rights Campaign is the first political action group working for equal rights for the LGBTQ community. This organization has lots of information on legal issues concerning transgender people.

LGBTQ Nation

www.lgbtqnation.com

This is a news website sharing news stories relevant to the LGBTQ community. The site also has a section for stories directly related to transgender people.

National Center for Transgender Equality

www.transequality.org

The National Center for Transgender Equality is an activist group located in Washington, DC. Founded in 2005 by trans rights activists, the center advocates for the rights of transgender people around the country.

PFLAG
www.pflag.org

PFLAG, which originally stood for Parents and Friends of Lesbians and Gays, offers support and services for all LGBTQ people and their families, including the transgender community. The organization began in 1978 with a mother choosing to publicly support her gay son.

them.
www.them.us

This website calls itself a next-generation news site. It offers news and entertainment through an LGBTQ lens. The bright and colorful website is navigated through an Instagram-style scroll.

Transgender Law Center
www.transgenderlawcenter.org

Founded in 2002, the Transgender Law Center provides legal assistance to transgender people. It is both trans run and trans focused. The center has litigated for positive changes for transgender people at work, at school, in housing, in prison, and throughout society.

Trans Justice Funding Project
www.transjusticefundingproject.org

This organization seeks to promote and support trans grassroots initiatives run by and for transgender people. A panel of six people reviews applications and provides funding for community-based organizations to complete projects supporting transgender people.

Trans Student Educational Resources
www.transstudent.org

This is a youth-led organization providing advocacy resources for transgender youth. Its goal is to create trans-friendly schools and provide trans activists with the tools needed to be effective organizers.

For Further Research

Books

Lee Airton, *Gender: Your Guide*. Avon, MA: Adams Media, 2019.

Jaimee Garbacik, *Gender and Sexuality for Beginners*. Danbury, CT: For Beginners, 2013.

Sally Hines, *Is Gender Fluid?* New York: Thames & Hudson, 2018.

Kris Hirschmann, *Understanding Sexual Identity and Orientation*. San Diego, CA: ReferencePoint, 2018.

Susan Kuklin, *Beyond Magenta: Transgender Teens Speak Out*. Somerville, MA: Candlewick, 2015.

Barbara Sheen, *LGBTQ in America*. San Diego, CA: Reference Point, 2021.

Internet Sources

Bethany Ao, "Transgender People with IDs That Match Their Gender Have Better Mental Health, Drexel Study Finds," *Philadelphia (PA) Inquirer*, March 24, 2020. www.inquirer.com.

Liz Entman, "Transgender Americans Experience Significant Economic, Health Challenges: Study," Vanderbilt University, April 13, 2020. https://news.vanderbilt.edu.

"Gender Dysphoria," *Psychology Today*, February, 23, 2019. www.psychologytoday.com.

Dan Levin, "A Clash Across America over Transgender Rights," *New York Times*, March 12, 2020. www.nytimes.com.

Julie Moreau, "Year After Trans Military Ban, Legal Battle Rages," NBC News, April 11, 2020. www.nbcnews.com.

Sara Reardon, "The Largest Study Involving Transgender People Is Providing Long-sought Insights About Their Health," *Nature*, April 24, 2019. www.nature.com.

Alanna Vagianos, "At Least 22 Transgender People Were Killed In 2019. Here Are Their Stories," HuffPost, November 20, 2019. www.huffpost.com.

Lucas Waldron and Brenda Medina, "When Transgender Travelers Walk into Scanners, Invasive Searches Sometimes Wait on the Other Side," ProPublica and *Miami (FL) Herald*, August 26, 2019. www.propublica.org.

Ed Yong, "Young Trans Children Know Who They Are," *Atlantic*, January 15, 2019. www.theatlantic.com.

Index

use of laws against sex-based discrimination, 55–57

environment as cause of gender dysphoria, 24–25

estrogen, 32, 40–42

Fair Housing Act, 59

family
increase in knowledge about gender diversity, 14–15
negative reactions of, 17–19, 20, 36
PFLAG and, 70
positive reactions of, 17, 36, 39–40
religion and, 55
understanding of gender-diverse individuals as children, 10

FBI, 49–50

female-to-male hormone treatment, 43–44

female-to-male surgeries, **47**, 47–48

gender
biological sex and, 6, 11
cisgender, 7, 11
elements of, 6
as social construct, 29–33
as spectrum or mosaic, 6–9, 21, 29–30

gender-affirming surgeries.

See surgical transitioning

gender binary, 6, 11–12, 29

gender diversity
chemical exposure and, 32
feeling of being different, 10
as function of biology, 23, 26, 29
increase in parents' knowledge about, 14–15
as psychological disorder, 22–24
as result of how raised, 24–25

gender dysphoria
described, 12, 41
gender identity disorder changed to, 22
potential effects of, 12–13
depression, 14, 25, 32, 33–34
eating disorders, 33
self-esteem issues, 14
See also suicide
self-realization, 15–16

gender expression, 29–33, **30**

gender fluid identification, 12

gender identity, 6–9

gender nonbinary, 12

gender policing, 44

Gibson, Elliot, 16

GLAAD, 68

hair changes with transitioning, 41, **42**, 43

Picture Credits

About the Author

Olivia Ghafoerkhan has an MFA in writing for children and young adults from Hamline University. She is the author of several non-fiction books for teens and young readers. She teaches college composition in Northern Virginia, where she lives with her family.